Contents

Weblink: www.curriculumvisions.com

Food

Our food can be put into groups.
There are five food groups.

Group 1 Vegetables

These are plants that we normally cook and eat with our meals, or have with salads.

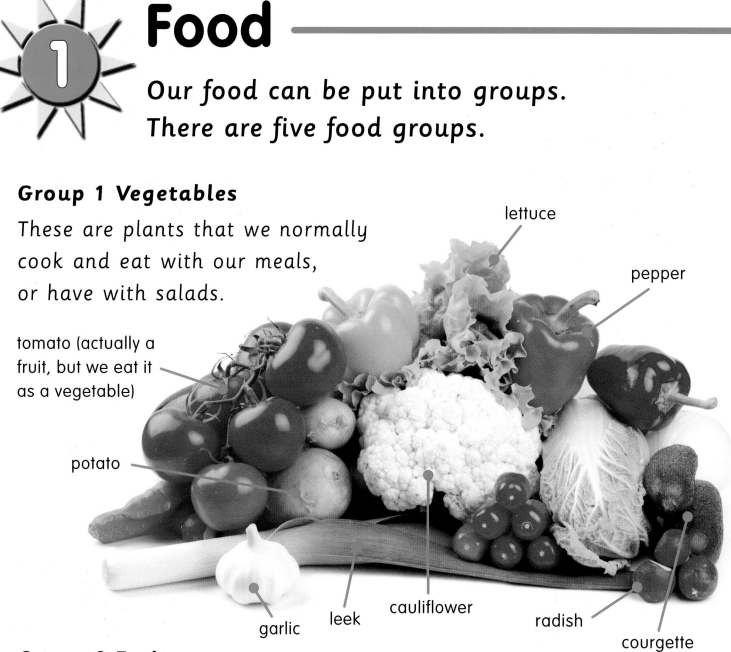

lettuce

pepper

tomato (actually a fruit, but we eat it as a vegetable)

potato

garlic

leek

cauliflower

radish

courgette

Group 2 Fruit

We eat fruit after a meal or between meals.
It includes bananas, oranges, peaches and apples.

cherry

grape

orange

peach

kiwifruit

4

Health and growth

Pete op

Curriculum Visions

Science@School

Teacher's Guide
There is a Teacher's Guide available to accompany this book.

Dedicated Web Site
There is a wealth of supporting material including videos and activities available at the Professional Zone, part of our dedicated web site:

www.CurriculumVisions.com

The Professional Zone
is a subscription zone.

A CVP Book.
First published in 2008

Copyright © 2008 Earthscape

Authors
Peter Riley, BSc, C Biol, MI Biol, PGCE, and Brian Knapp, BSc, PhD

Senior Designer
Adele Humphries, BA, PGCE

Educational Consultant
Jan Smith (former Deputy Head of Wellfield School, Burnley, Lancashire)

Editor
Gillian Gatehouse

Designed and produced by
EARTHSCAPE

Printed in China by
WKT Co., Ltd

Curriculum Visions Science@School
Volume 2A Health and growth
A CIP record for this book is available from the British Library.
ISBN: 978 1 86214 259 6

Picture credits
All pictures are from the Earthscape and ShutterStock collections.

This product is manufactured from sustainable managed forests. For every tree cut down at least one more is planted.

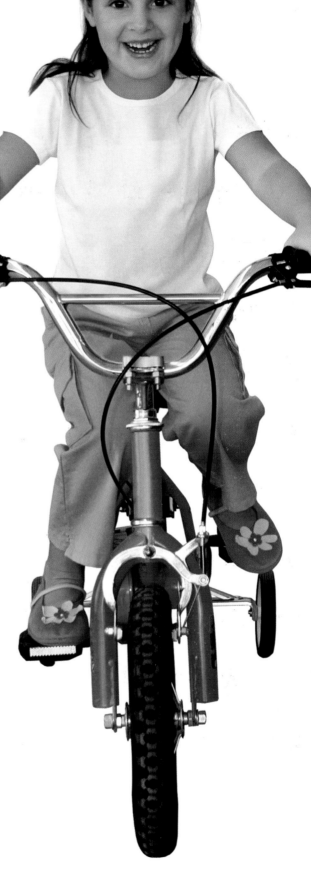

Exercise is good for your health.

Group 3 Cereals

This includes rice, pasta and bread. Bread and pasta are made from a cereal called wheat.

bread

pasta

rice

Group 4 Meat

Includes chicken, lamb, fish and eggs.

fish

meat

egg

cheese

milk

Group 5 Dairy products

These are milk, cream, cheese, butter and yoghurt.

Can you think of more foods to put in each group?

Weblink: www.curriculumvisions.com

2 Why we need food

We need food to keep us well, to give us energy and to help us grow.

1. Keeping healthy

Fruit and vegetables help fight off disease.

2. Giving energy

We need food to give us energy. We get lots of energy from cereals like wheat, and vegetables like potatoes. Sugar and fat also give us energy.

A field of barley. Barley is a cereal.

watermelon

Weblink: www.curriculumvisions.com

3. Helping us grow

Meat, fish, eggs and dairy products help us to grow.

Some vegetables, like peas and beans, also help us to grow.

Growing up needs food.

If we do not eat, we get hungry. That is our body telling us it is time to eat. If we do not eat for days, we become very tired. If we do not eat properly for weeks, we may start to get diseases. This is because we will not be able to keep germs away.

What might happen if we do not eat fruit and vegetables?

Weblink: www.curriculumvisions.com

3 Healthy meals

We must eat balanced meals if we are to keep healthy.

We need to eat some of most of these – vegetables, fruit, cereals, meat and dairy products – if we are to stay healthy.

pizza

cheese

Look at this pizza. It is made from vegetables as well as pasta (cereal) and meat. It has a cheese (dairy) topping.

Weblink: www.curriculumvisions.com

cream and chocolate cake

Some foods, such as sweets, cakes and chocolate, have lots of sugar in them. Sugar gives us energy, but too much of it will make us fat.

pie with tomato ketchup

Some foods have lots of fat, sugar and salt. These are mostly foods we buy already cooked. Crisps, pies, chips and ready-meals are some of these.

It is fine to eat a little of these kinds of food, but if we eat them all of the time we will have so much salt and fat that it will be bad for us.

potato crisps

Do you eat healthy meals?

9

Drinking

We need water as well as food to keep healthy. When our body needs water it makes us feel thirsty.

Our body is mostly made up of water. Our blood has water in it, so does our skin and muscles.

Our bodies also use water to get rid of parts of our food that we don't need to keep.

The body loses water when we sweat and when we go to the toilet.

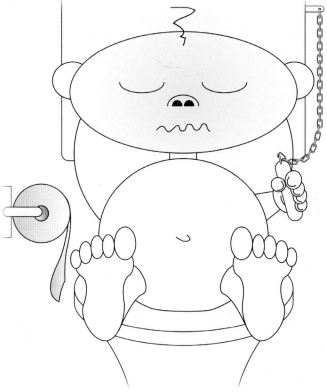

We lose water when we go to the toilet.

We put water back by drinking.

If we drink more than the body needs, we get rid of it by going to the toilet. But if we don't drink enough, the body holds on to what it has and doesn't flush the nasty substances away. This might make us ill.

Weblink: www.curriculumvisions.com

Fizzy drinks have water in, but also a lot of sugar.

Fruit squash has water in, but little sugar.

There is water in everything we drink – in fizzy drinks, in squash, in milk, in tea and coffee.

What is important is that we drink lots of water.

Milk has water in.

How many different kinds of drink do you drink?

Weblink: www.curriculumvisions.com

5

Exercise

When we exercise we make our muscles strong and keep our bodies fit.

Just as a rusty old bike is more difficult to get going than a well-oiled one, so a fit body is more healthy than one that is unfit.

We keep our bodies in tip-top health by working them hard. This means doing exercise.

If we don't exercise, our heart, leg and arm muscles get weak. A weak heart muscle is dangerous for our health.

Any running game is good exercise.

Riding a bicycle exercises our legs and our heart.

Dancing exercises our legs and our hearts.

Swimming exercises all of the body.

What exercise do you take to keep fit and healthy?

How do you feel after taking exercise?

Weblink: www.curriculumvisions.com

Babies and toddlers

As babies grow into toddlers they change what they do.

Babies are very small and weak. They need food to help them grow up. Their legs are too weak to let them stand. They cannot speak to us when they are uncomfortable and so they cry.

They wriggle.

They cry.

They need lots of sleep.

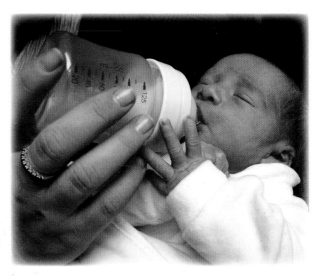
They only have milk for food.

Weblink: www.curriculumvisions.com

Toddlers eat lots of different foods.

Toddlers need less sleep than babies.

When babies grow strong enough to walk they are called toddlers. Toddlers can get about. They know how to use their hands. They can also talk and tell us what they want and when they are not happy.

Toddlers walk and talk.

How do babies and toddlers look different?

Weblink: www.curriculumvisions.com

Growing animals

Some young animals look like their parents, but many look very different.

All animals have young. We call our young people babies. Babies look much like grown-ups, but smaller.

Many young animals look like smaller grown-ups, too. Here is a baby cat. It is called a kitten. A baby dog is called a puppy and looks like a grown-up dog.

Kittens look like small cats.

Puppies look like grown-up dogs.

Weblink: www.curriculumvisions.com

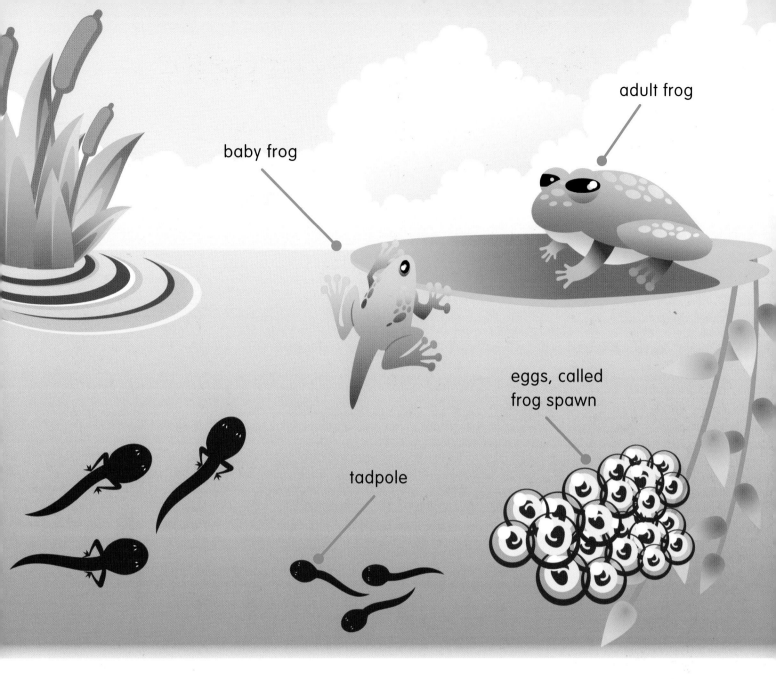

baby frog

adult frog

eggs, called frog spawn

tadpole

Some young animals do not look like the grown-ups. They live very different lives. A tadpole is a young frog. It begins life as an egg. When it hatches it looks like a black fish with a large head and a tail. It stays in the water and breathes like a fish.

As it grows up it gets legs. It loses its tail and then looks like a little frog. It now breathes air and lives out of the water.

What other animals have young which look like small adults?

Germs

Sometimes we can hurt ourselves or become ill. Germs are often the cause of illness.

Germs are tiny living things that are in the air, in the water, and sometimes on things we touch. Germs are too small for us to see. Some of them can make us ill.

Our bodies normally fight germs, but if we cut ourselves, germs can get into our bodies more easily. We wash the cut and put a plaster on to keep germs out until the cut has healed.

Putting a plaster on, and using antiseptic cream as soon as possible, keeps out germs.

Some germs spread when people cough and sneeze. We then breathe the germs in.

Weblink: www.curriculumvisions.com

If germs attack our bodies, the body fights back.

The body can do this more easily if it is hot. This is why we feel hot when we are ill, and sometimes we begin to sweat.

A thermometer helps tell how hot we are.

Washing hands is a good way of keeping germs away.

How do you feel when you are ill? Hot? Tired? In pain? Sick?

Weblink: www.curriculumvisions.com

Medicines

People sometimes take medicines when they are ill. But this must be done with care.

Some medicines are liquids you take from a spoon.

The body is usually very good at looking after itself. Sometimes it cannot cope with some kinds of germs and then it needs the help of medicines.

Medicines are special substances that scientists have made. They are used to help the body get over its illness.

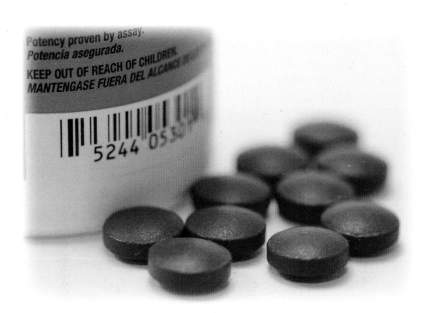

Most medicine containers have lots of writing on them. They are the instructions for grown-ups to read.

Some medicines are tablets.
They are different sizes,
shapes and colours.

Some medicines have to be
breathed in with an inhaler.

protective wrapper

tablet

inhaler

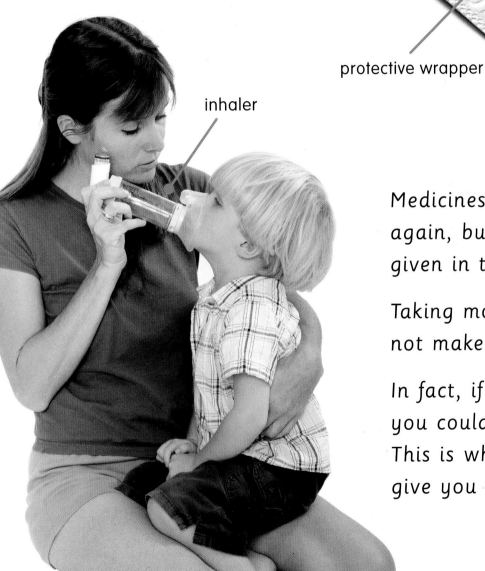

Medicines can make people well
again, but only when they are
given in the right amount.

Taking more than the dose will
not make you get better faster.

In fact, if you have too much
you could get even more ill.
This is why a grown-up must
give you your dose of medicine.

Who do you think should give you medicine?

Weblink: www.curriculumvisions.com

Words to learn

Adults

Grown-ups.

Antiseptic cream

A cream that kills germs.

Balanced meal

A meal with different foods to keep us healthy.

Cereals

Wheat, rice, barley, oats.

Dairy products

Milk, cheese, yoghurt, butter.

Weblink: www.curriculumvisions.com

Disease

Something which stops the body working properly and makes us feel ill.

Dose

The safe amount of medicine you can have at one time.

Energy

Something in food which makes us active.

Salad

A dish of cold, raw, vegetables that are chopped up.

Thermometer

An instrument that measures temperature.

Weblink: www.curriculumvisions.com

Index

Weblink: www.curriculumvisions.com